CHAPTER ONE
HOPES AND DREAMS

HOPES AND DREAMS

WHAT WOULD YOU WANT YOUR LIFE TO LOOK LIKE?

It's never too early or late to dream up your best life. Visualise where you would like to see yourself in the future. Where would you live, in a big city or perhaps in a private island? How would you spend your time and with who? What nice things do you want to own?

Everyone in life has had a dream - a dream of what they would want to become. Sadly, the majority of people give up: they grow up becoming grumpy and have to settle for unhappy, non-fulfilling lives. However, there are some who dream big: to be famous singers, athletes, businessmen, role models, leaders and they actually achieve it!

How? There are two life skills no one can avoid. The fact that you are reading and set on completing this book makes you one of the winners. Mind management, the way we perceive ourselves and situations makes a huge difference. They determine whether your dream will just be a dream or whether it will become a reality.

Financial management is very important. Remember that money cannot buy everything like love and acceptance, but it can buy experiences, a comfortable standard of living and it funds your dreams! Whether we like to admit it or not, money is super important.

DREAM CHASERS

This book is for the dreamers,
the achievers, and the future world leaders.
I have woven stories, lessons and quotes,
to empower my readers to reach for the stars!
I believe that anything is possible
if you put your mind to it.
Good speed ahead

THIS BOOK BELONGS TOO

_____

_____

TABLE OF CONTENTS

CHAPTER ONE: Hopes and Dreams
- 1.1 Hopes and Dreams
- 1.2 What is success?
- 1.3 Goals

CHAPTER TWO: Wise Money
- 2.1 What is money
- 2.2 Goods vs Services
- 2.3 Needs vs Wants
- 2.4 Income and Expenses

CHAPTER THREE: Mind Managemnt
- 3.1 My Mind
- 3.2 Habits
- 3.3 Acceptance

CHAPTER FOUR: Money Success
- 4.1 Investing
- 4.2 Savings account
- 4.3 Compound interest vs Simple interest
- 4.4 Credit and Interest
- 4.5 Invention vs Innovation
- 4.6 Negotiation
- 4.7 What is your Net worth?
- 4.8 Tax

CHAPTER FIVE: SETBACKS
- 5.1 Sad reasons why people give up
- 5.2 Persistence

WHAT IS SUCCESS?

Being successful is different for every person. One may define success as becoming a football player, while someone else will define success as giving a lot of stray dogs a loving home.

Letting other people, including parents, tell us what we must do to become successful is not our dream; but someone else's. Having one dream and goal is simply not enough, When you put your mind to it, you can be a superstar! For example, do you define success as being a successful Youtuber but end up having bad health problems? No, the trick is to have all areas of your life going well.

SO, STOP AND THINK FOR A MOMENT AND DEFINE SUCCESS TO YOU

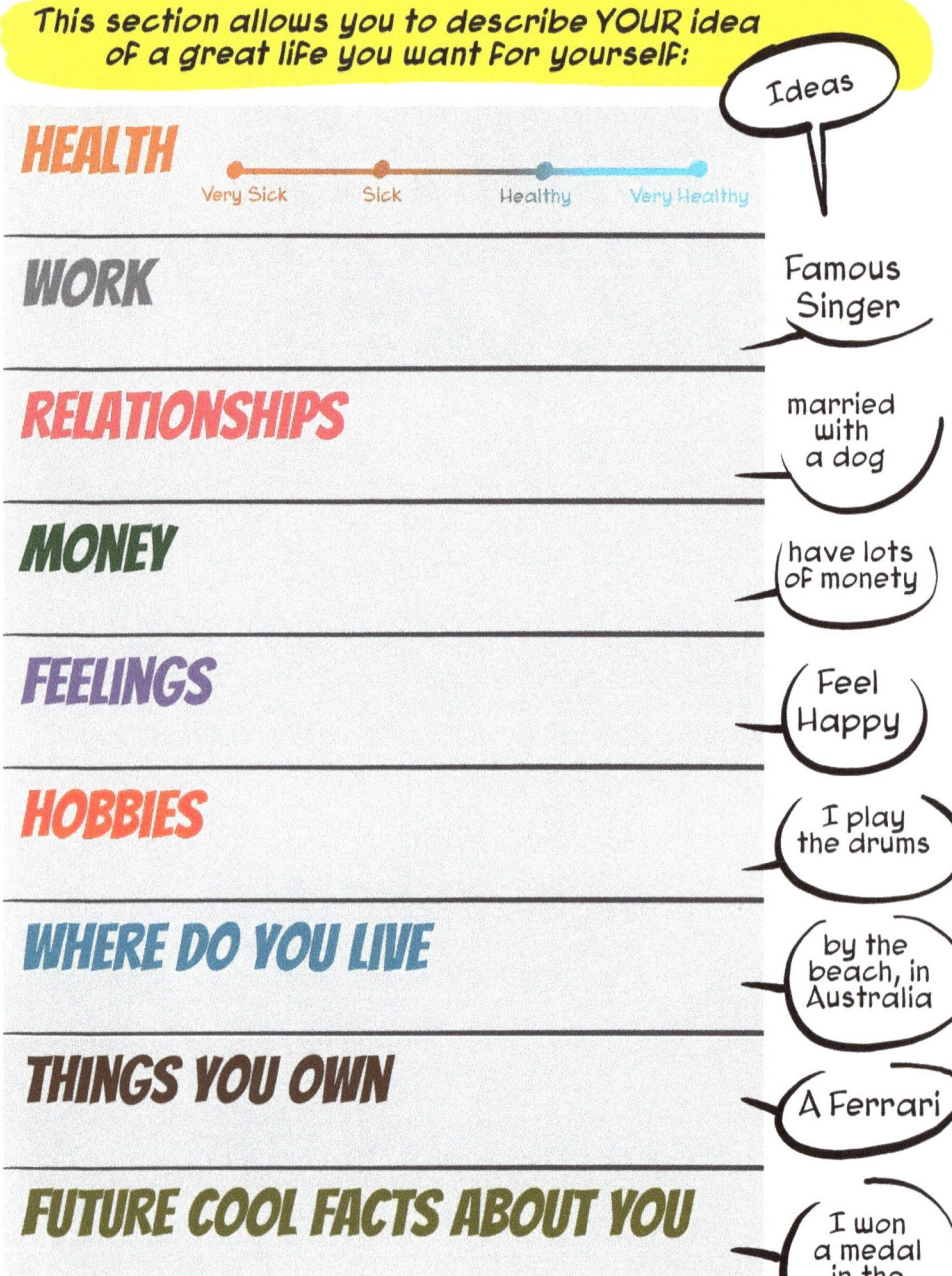

5 years, 10 years, 20 years or 40 years.
I WILL be ___ old

Write what you will do
in your week in __ years' time.

You may work on your passion a few days a week and keep the rest for hobbies and fun?
It's your life, dream it up

Sunday		
Monday	Tuesday	Wednesday
Thursday	Friday	Saturday

Remember, everyone's skills, interests and aspirations do change over time

What are some of the great things about you?

What do people like and admire about you?

What do you like about yourself?

What are you good at?

What are your skills, abilities and talents?

Great things about me

What are some positive things people say about you?

What I'm good at?

GOALS

A dream written down with a date becomes a goal.

A goal broken down into steps becomes a Plan.

A plan backed by action becomes reality.

You are 42 percent more likely to achieve your goals if you write them down. Writing your goals down not only forces you to get clear on what exactly it is that you want to accomplish, but doing so plays a part in motivating you to achieve your dream.

Now that you have dreams written down, (remember dreams can change over time) it's time to look at goals. Goals give a sense of purpose and direction, it makes us feel fulfilled and happy when we have achieved our goals. To get to a far away exciting place you have never been before, you could get lost, right? However, using a map or GPS ensure you get there. Think of goals as your own Map/GPS that you always have with you.

Your goal maybe is to make a 1 million dollar invention. How do you achieve your goal?

You have to start small, then work your way up. Like walking up the stairs, you take one step up. Then another, then another step. After several steps, you are at the top! It took time and effort but now you're at the top.

Bill Gates, the second richest man in the world, whose dream was to improve the world with his software had to do it slowly by using small goals.

Fact studies show only 8% of people achieve their New Year's resolution! So, while your dreams should be insanely big, your goals to get that dream should be small and achievable. Once you achieve them, you get a happy feeling called satisfaction.

Dream *(top of the stairs)*

If our dream is to get fortune and fame by having 1 million subscribers on YouTube, we need a broken down plan:

Goals Broken Down

1. Create a plan on what type of videos you want to make
2. Learn about editing, camera angles, sounds and technical stuff
3. Watch videos which will be similar to the ones you want to make
4. Record your video
5. Edit/ upload video
6. Gain subscribers and do marketing work to get subscribers
7. Work hard by putting out more content
8. Goal achieved

This all may seem like very hard work – an impossible task. However, when you break down your goal into smaller steps, you get a sense of satisfaction that keeps you going. That feeling of accomplishment and satisfaction is worth a lot more than money because it is a goal towards your dream. A dream that you achieved because you are special!

DREAM = REALITY

Here are 5 staircases
Write down your dream at the top,
then climb your way up with your goals.

step one
step two
step three
step four

Many people fail in their goals because they don't take the time to think of what problems they may encounter. Every goal has a few obstacles that can send you off track. When dieting people often have a day when they may indulge in food that is not on their 'list' of approved food. Think doughnuts. So, they made a mistakes and ate a doughnut in the morning.

Such a misstep often sends dieters into a tailspin. They make more bad food choices because they feel bad about the first, and slowly begin working their way off their diet. However, with an if, then statement "IF I make a bad food choice, THEN I will immediately get back on track," there will be no blaming because you have planned for this eventuality.

What are some positive qualities about you that will help you reach your goals

What might get in the way of you reaching your goals?

How will you monitor your progress towards your goal? (i.e. sticker chart)

List all the things you are weak at,

"A goal without a plan is just a wish"

Write what thoughts and feelings come up when you read this quote

WHAT IS MONEY?

"The more you learn the more you earn". So let's learn about money.

Money is a 'medium of exchange' between humans on earth which means you can exchange 'money' for goods like toys, cars, books or services such as getting a haircut.

In ancient times before money was invented, humans would 'barter'. This means that people would trade goods and services for other goods and services. For example, a farmer with eggs and milk can trade them with a local baker for a birthday cake and a loaf of bread. The baker then uses the milk and eggs to bake more bread and exchanges it with a builder who builds her a house.

The bartering system was so normal that even after the invention of money, people still preferred to barter. The problem was that there was no way of putting an exact value on things we have today.

If you had lemons, one day you may be able to trade it for something very valuable, but the next day you may get something not so valuable. The other problem was if you had many t-shirts and you wanted to barter them for some new shoes, however no one wanted your t-shirts, you would be stuck. Hence money or gold coins became so popular because you can exchange it for various things.

Roman soldiers would get paid in salt and Europeans would barter fur coats and perfumes. Early Americans would trade wheat.

Currency symbols are different in other countries.
Draw your currency symbol here:

You can find plenty of stories about superstar athletes and big-name singers, rich businessmen who were earning millions but ended up broke. So, it is very important that you don't just make money but keep it. It's unwise to let people 'handle your money' for you. They could steal your hard-earned money.

HOW CAN I EARN MONEY?

There are many things you can do to earn money. The key, however, is finding the things that appeal to your likes and interests. If you don't really like dogs, you probably shouldn't start a dog walking business even if your best friend makes a lot of money doing it in her neighbourhood. You'll need to spend some time thinking about the things you like to do and how you can turn that into a money-making job.

Write Your Interests
4 ways I can make money from my interest

1. _____
2. _____
3. _____
4. _____

List all of the things you are interested in and all the things you are good at

How can these interests and skills make you money?

Example Interest = drawing

1. Draw your cartoon characters include story lines and send the idea to animation studios you may is the owner of the next Pokemon, One Piece, Ben 10
2. Become an illustrator for books and magazines
3. Become a famous artist selling your art for hundreds of thousands
4. Become an architect designing beautiful structures

Ask your parents to help you think of ways your interests can make you money. They are older and know more about the world.

Read how these people transformed their hobbies and talents into very successful lives.

Debbi Fields

Debbi Fields loved baking. cookies in particular - it brought here joy. She was not discouraged even if she was so poor and couldn't always afford real ingredients Debbie used the next best thing, replacing butter or margarine and sometimes using imitation chocolate.

Debbie's interest in baking cookies developed a highly successful cookie empire. That is now worth $450 million!

Michael J. Kittredge

Struggling to find a Christmas gift for his mom. Michael then aged 16 was creative and talented enough to melt red crayons into a candle. Kittredge started making candles in his parents' garage and selling them at his school. By age 20 Michael launched Yankee Candles. He then rented a small workspace producing more candles. Ten years later he opened up a huge factory and in 2013 the company was sold for 1.75 billion.

Mark Zuckerberg

Mark was interested in computers, practically coding. While in university, he started a small social media website, just for students on campus. It was just a hobby a side project which ultimately became Facebook which blossomed into a multibillion-dollar global company. Today, his net worth is estimated to be just under $70 billion, making him the 7th richest person in the world.

Now that you've written down several career possibilities pick one that sounds the best for you right now. Imagine how far it could take you one day. Think big! Would you become the next Olympian, award winning actress or the next billionaire inventor?

Pretend you are being interviewed in the future about your successful life. (This exercise will get you to speak as if it has already happened, which is a great little mind trick to help your brain bring positive energy and a good sense of direction on what you want to happen in life.)

Now that you've written down several career possibilities, pick one that sounds the best for you right now. Imagine how far it could take you one day. Think big! Would you become...

the next Olympian, award winning actress or the next billionaire inventor?

Pretend you are being interviewed in the future about your successful life. (This exercise will get you to speak as if it has already happened, which is a great little mind trick to help your brain bring positive energy and a good sense of direction on what you want to happen in life.)

INTERVIEWER QUESTIONS

WHAT HAVE YOU DONE?
_____
_____
_____
_____

HOW DO YOU KEEP ACHIEVING, WHEN SETBACKS HAPPEN?
_____
_____
_____
_____

WHY HAVE YOU PICKED THIS PATH?
_____
_____
_____
_____

WHEN DID YOU KNOW YOU WANTED TO DO THIS?
_____
_____
_____
_____

GOODS VS SERVICES

If you want to be successful, you need to have an understanding of our minds. You will also need an understanding of money as it is a precious resource you will need for the rest of your life, no matter what you do. Very little is learnt about money in school. So, let's learn more knowledge and skills about money, to give you an extra edge on being a success.

We spend our money on two things: **goods** or a **service**.

A good is something that is tangible. It's an item that can be held or touched. (Examples include toys, bikes, furniture, cars, machinery, plants, etc.)

A service is work performed for others. (Examples could be the dentist, dry cleaners, dog walkers, realtors, etc.)

Everything for sale falls under one of these two categories. People make money at their jobs by selling either a good or a service.

Everyone with a job works for an income. Income is the amount you are paid for doing your work. Think of some of your adult relatives. Do they have jobs? Is there jobs goods or service based?

(Service or goods)

Mum works in _____ industry

Dad works in _____ industry

ARE THESE GOODS OR SERVICE?

1. You get your hair cut.
_____

2. You buy a book from a garage sale.
_____

3. You buy your mother a flower from a flower shop.
_____

4. You hire someone to cut your lawn.
_____

5. You visit the doctor for a check-up.
_____

6. You purchase a game to give as a birthday gift.
_____

7. You pay your sister $5 to clean your messy bedroom.
_____

Answers: 1. service, 2. good, 3. good, 4. service, 5. service, 6. good, 7. service.

Some businesses provide only goods, while others provide only services. However, many businesses provide some mixture of the two. Example a garage door company might sell garage doors (a good) but might also send people out to repair your existing door (a service).

NEEDS VS WANTS

Money helps feed you, and clothe you. Money allows you to purchase gifts for yourself as well as others and pays for experiences you would otherwise not have like travel, sports events, higher education, etc. So, we spend our money on either goods or services but they can also be either needs or wants.

NEEDS: FOOD, SHELTER, SECURITY

WANTS: IMPULSE BUYS

NEEDS ARE SOMETHING YOU MUST HAVE FOR SURVIVAL. FOR EXAMPLE, FOOD AND WATER. WITHOUT FOOD, YOU WOULD NOT BE ABLE TO LIVE.

WANTS ARE SOMETHING THAT YOU WOULD LIKE TO HAVE, BUT IT IS NOT NECESSARY, AND YOU COULD DO WITHOUT IT. AN EXAMPLE WOULD BE ENTERTAINMENT, TOYS, CDS, ETC.

Sometimes needs and wants overlap. For example, cake is a food. However it is not a need, but a want. In general, you need a basic diet to survive, but that diet does not need to include cake.

List your Wants and Needs Below:

Needs:
_____
_____
_____
_____
_____
_____

Wants:
_____
_____
_____
_____
_____
_____

INCOME AND EXPENSES

We spend money on goods and services and also things like charity. We also invest our money to make more. There is a saying, "if you want to become rich you have to spend money to make money." This is called expenses. When parents purchase groceries, or when businesses spend money on supplies, they are all called expenses.

Expenses don't have to be just about purchasing goods. An expense could also be the amount you want to put into savings every week. It could also be money that you wish to give away to charity. As long as the money is going out, it is an expense.

There are two main types of expense: **Fixed expenses and variable expenses.**

Fixed expenses tend to be about the same each week or month, for example rent.

Variable expenses tend to change each week or month, such as clothing and food.

Tick which you think is a fixed or variable expense

EXPENSES FIXED VARIABLE	FIXED	VARIABLE
Rent/Mortgage		
Utilities (water+ electricity bill)		
Groceries/Food		
Clothing		
Fuel		
Entertainment		
TV Subscription Service		

Answers: Fixed, variable, variable, variable, variable, variable, Fixed

Many adults get into a lot of trouble in life because their expenses are a lot higher than their income. It is easy to know exactly how much you need for fixed expenses. However variable and unexpected expenses like expensive medicine when you get sick is hard to calculate. Income is also not always guaranteed. You may lose your job or in some jobs like being an entrepreneur you may make very little money that week.

It is very important to always have savings tucked away for emergencies. "Save for a rainy day" Smart people always have savings. There is a saying,

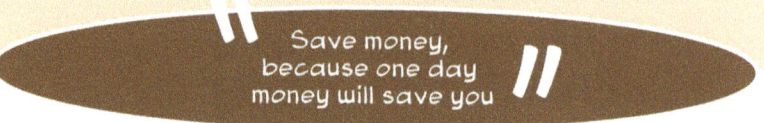

" Save money, because one day money will save you "

Fill out the table below using the expenses Christopher tracked. Then total fixed and variable expenses. Also calculate total expenses.

Expenses: House Mortgage payment $245, Electricity bill $65, Food shopping $96, New coat $51, TV Subscription service $24, going to the movies $39, Fuel $48

Category	Fixed	Variable
EXPENSES:		
Rent/Mortgage	$245	
Utilities (Electricity)		$
Groceries/Food		$
Clothing		$
Fuel		$
Entertainment		$
TV Subcription Service	$	
EXPENSES SUBTOTAL	$	+ $
TOTAL EXPENSES (Fixed + Variable)	= $	

Answers: Fixed = 269, Variable = 299, Total 568

So, each month Chris expenses are $568 meaning he must earn OVER $568 per month. After these expenses are paid Chris must put money away in savings away for a rainy day.

"SAVE MONEY AND ONE DAY IT WILL SAVE YOU"

Circle the correct answer for each question.

1	Wise shoppers take time to compare two or three alternatives before spending money.	True	False
2	Taking time to read about discounts at shops can save money when shopping.	True	False
3	We can look at advertisements and learn how they make us want an item.	True	False
4	My needs should take priority over my wants when shopping.	True	False
5	Television commercials for food products are always factual.	True	False

6. Television adverts influence spending decisions by:
- a. using special music
- b. using pretty pictures
- c. making me think I need the item
- d. all of the above

7. A spending need is:
- a. something that looks good to me
- b. something that I need to exist
- c. something my friend has
- d. the first thing I see in the store

8. The best spending choice is:
- a. always shop at Brand-name stores
- b. buy the same thing my friends buy
- c. compare my choices before I buy
- d. always borrow from friends

Answers: 1. True 2. True 3. True 4. True 5. False 6. d 7. b 8. c

MY MIND

In Superhero Movies there is always a good guy like Batman and Spiderman. Then there is always a villain like Joker or Magneto. Did you know your mind is the same? You can give power to either the superhero to make it stronger or the bad guy.

How?

Self-talk. We tell ourselves "I hate myself" or "I suck at sports". Over time we start to believe these thoughts.
Soon one negative self-thought becomes more and more.
Then we don't believe in ourselves and are certain our dreams will not happen.

It is perfectly normal to think of negative thoughts, but we don't want to give too much to our villain inside. We want our superhero to win

Science shows that successful people give a lot more power to their inner superhero through positive self-talk, saying things like, "I'm good at thinking of solutions" and "I will overcome this problem."

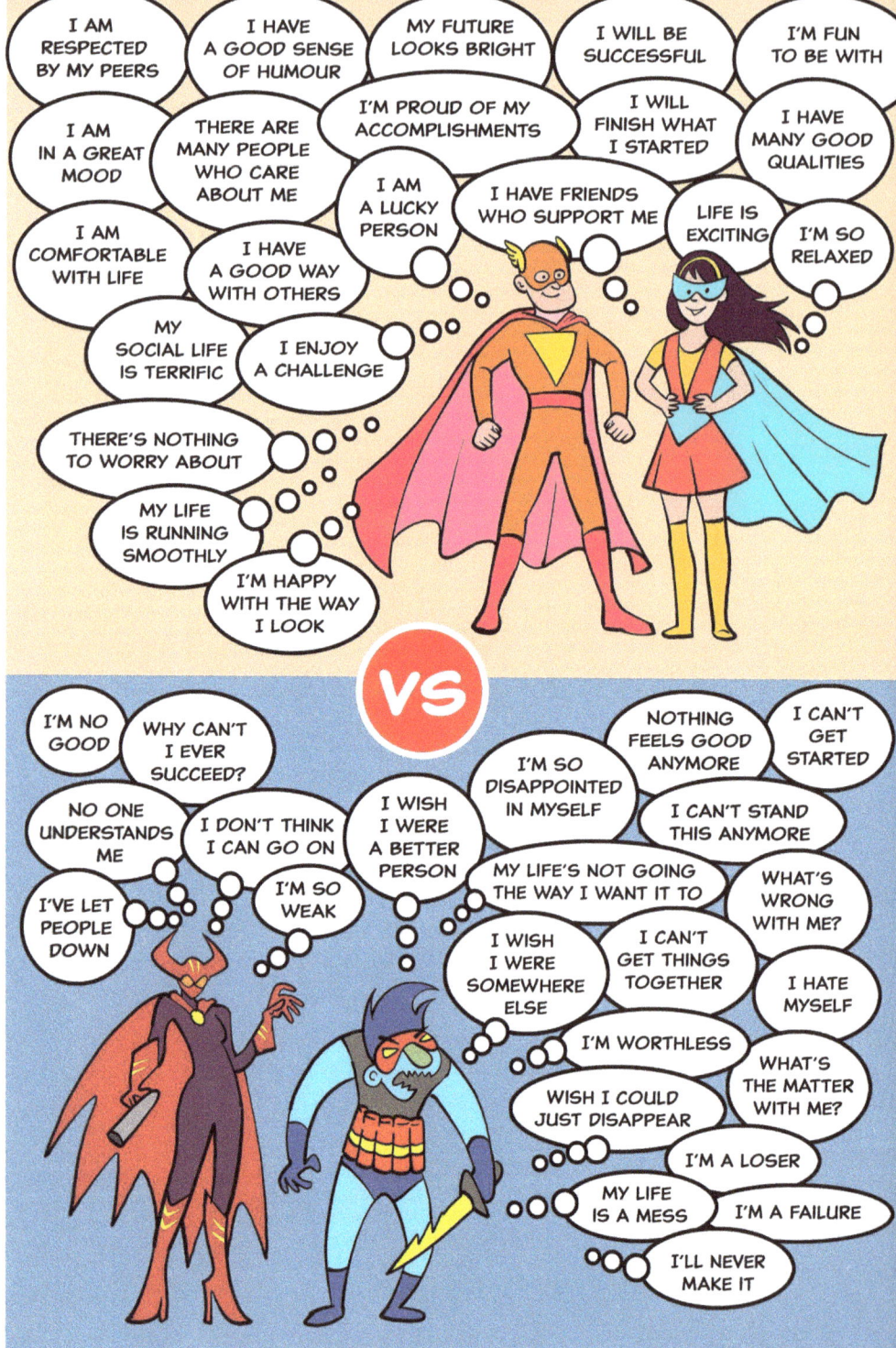

How much power does your inner superhero already have?
Circle the number that comes to your mind immediately,
the highest being most likely.

"I'm always going to be bad at things I do"	1	2	3	4	5
"My life is always going to be disappointing"	1	2	3	4	5
"What's the matter with me? Everyone hates me"	1	2	3	4	5
You believe "you will always be unintelligent" compared to others	1	2	3	4	5
I will never achieve my dreams	1	2	3	4	5

SCORE

5 - 10 your inner superhero is really positive

11 - 20 your mind needs improvement and might hold you back in life.

21 - 30 your villain is winning and holding you back

Positive self-talk boosts confidence, helps you achieve anything, gets you through challenging times no matter how big the problem is, increases life expectancy, makes you feel happier and enables you to achieve your dreams

Negative self-talk -- makes you stressed, stops you from achieving your dreams, you lose friends

"POSITIVE THOUGHTS GENERATE POSITIVE FEELINGS AND CREATE POSITIVE RESULTS"

Core belief

All actions start from a thought,
and thoughts are affected by outside influences.

For example, if everyone says you are a bad person it becomes your core belief. Something you believe to be true about yourself even though it's not. When you turn your negative thoughts into positive it becomes your beliefs

What are some of the positive things people say about you?

What are things you say about yourself repeatedly,
These are your core beliefs

How the brain is effected

Every thought releases chemicals. When we think positive our brain releases serotonin (feel good chemical). Negative thoughts releases bad chemicals like cortisol which drains the brain's ability to function making us feel depressed, and unmotivated to achieve goals.

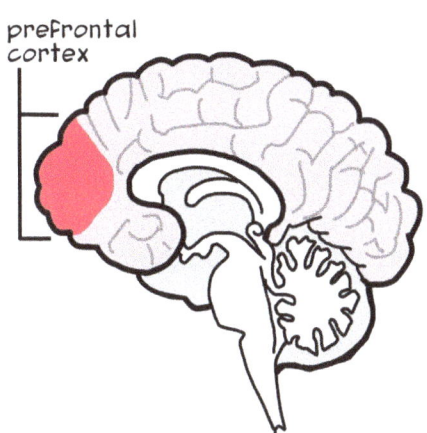

prefrontal cortex

The prefrontal cortex is in charge of our emotions. The left half being involved with positive feelings, and the right with negative ones. When you think positive thoughts there is brain growth.

If we break a bone, we are in pain for awhile, then the pain heals. However, mental pain caused by stressful situations and nasty words from peers, etc. Gets built into the mind deeper, therefore, we can re-live the pain in our minds over and over for a long time.

Since mental pain is built into our mind deeper, it's easy to get stuck in unhappiness. This is why people don't achieve their dream because they have not learnt to give.

How can we give more power to our superhero?
Perception!

Perception is how we understand or interpret something. For example,

Mary turned 40 years, at her birthday. She was crying because she felt old and disappointed.

Jay turned 40 years, he enjoyed his birthday because he was glad to have reached 40 years old! Knowing that some people don't get to live that long

Mary and Jay both turned 40; one stayed positive and happy to have made it to 40, while one was upset as her perception was 'she old' now. Even though they are at the same age, they perceived things differently

Take this story:

Michael was a boy who was cut from his high school basketball team. The coach said, "you aren't good enough!" Upset, Michael went home and cried. His first thoughts where "I'm not good enough' and "I should give up"

However, he chose not to let a setback affect him. He thought, 'Ok I'm bad at basketball right now, but I am going to practise every day and get really good at basketball!

He would use that disappointing feeling as motivation to try harder and harder by practicing his dribbling, shooting and rebound. Then one day that boy grew up to become MICHAEL JORDAN

Michael Jordan's inner villain became strong when he got cut from his high school team. His negative talk was saying he is not good enough. However, he gave power to his inner superhero, saying to himself 'I'm going to get better by practising'.

His perception was just because I am bad at something now does not mean I will be bad at it forever

Now-

Michael Jordan is the richest athlete of all time, worth 21 billion in assets.

Even after retiring from sports. Michael Jordan still gets passive income from royalties. Nike pays him $100 million per year!

- Describe one situation or memory that made you upset

_____
e.g. ("I wanted to make a cartoon series. But I gave up")
- What negative thoughts do you remember having at the time?

_____
e.g. (" I suck at drawing I can never make my own cartoon")
- How could you change your perception?.
  Turn that negative thought into a positive

_____
e.g. (" Now I know what area I want to improve on, which is drawing")
- What is another situation you can think of?
  Write it down Positive perception takes practice soon it will be automatic

_____

HABITS

So, we have identified having mind management skills and money management skills is important to lead successful lives.
How do we do both? Develop good habits.

Your inner superhero has good habits formed soon. now living a dream life

Your inner villain forms bad habits. Now is lonely, stressed and broke

What is a habit?
Habits is something we do regularly with consciously thinking much about it.

For example, when you get up you brush your teeth.
You don't put much though into it and now you have great teeth!

A bad habit will be forgetting to brush your teeth.
Now you have to get expensive fillings and become self-conscious because you have rotten teeth.

What are some bad habits you want to replace with good habits?
~~~~~~~~~~~~~~~~~~~~~~~~~~~

Circle which you already do

1. Get on a good schedule.
2. Eat a healthy diet.
3. Learn to exercise.
4. Practice gratitude.
5. Develop good study habits.
6. Never give up!
7. Manage money wisely.
8. Respect the environment.
9. Plan your future
11. Practice good hygiene.
12. Telling the truth
13. Ask for what you want.
14. Be a regular reader.
15. Being on time
16. Respect authority.

Can you list 3 others??

ACCEPTANCE

The primary difference between the wealthy and successful people and those who struggle is acceptance.

Snoop Dogg

Calvin Broadus dreamed one day of becoming something of himself. Life had not been good to Calvin. His father left when he was 3 months old. Grew up in one of Americas worst neighbourhoods; a lot of crime and negative influences around him. His mother would struggle to feed all three children. Calvin started hanging out with bad people and eventually going to jail for breaking the law.

However, Calvin decided he was not going to accept a below average life. Calvin still had a big dream to be a musician. Despite having extreme difficulties his childhood, he decided to work hard on his music. He used his difficult circumstances to achieve success. His songs talk about his struggles and his life.

Calvin grew up becoming Snoop Dogg one of the biggest selling musicians of all time. With fame and fortune Calvin definitely has enough spare time and money to do whatever brings him happiness.

Calvin decided he will NOT accept the fact that; life had not been kind to him. Regardless of things happening, that he had no control over such as not having a dad in his life. He realised that he was the only one who could his current life. He then he started to do something about it.

There were many people in Calvin's neighbourhood and life who had a similar sad story growing up. However, they chose to complain accepting 'life sucks' and chose to not do something about it. Just waiting passively to see what happens

Remember - "You will be waiting forever if you waiting for someone else to change your life for you"

What do you not like? How is your life is going at the moment?

_____

What are some things that you can do to change your life?

_____

Do I believe I can achieve this   or
Do I have all the skills I need to make this change?   or
if no what skills do I need

_____

INVESTING

You can save your money, but what about making it grow?
This is called investing, which is the best way to make yourself rich.

Before investing your money, you will have to understand the important concept of risk and return.

How much 'return' is worth the risk you take? For example, if you keep your money in your home, you risk that it could be lost or stolen. But if you place your money in a bank account, your money will be safer but you risk having low investment profits.

All investments have different amount of returns (profit) and different risk you have to take to get that returns.

Here is Peter and Bob,

PETER

BOB

- Peter likes taking a lot of risks.
  (If you invest in an opportunity with a lot of risk, then you should expect to get a higher return on investment)

- Bob doesn't like taking a lot of risk-
  (Low risk investments should give you a lower return on investment.)

- Peter loves risks, he invested $10,000 of his savings into a company that digs for gold. If they find gold, Peter will make 10 times his money- $100,000 per year

- Bob is safer; he decided to invest his $10,000 into a company that sells paper. He only estimated to make $2000 profit per year

- Unfortunately the company Peter invested in, didn't find gold so he lost his savings.

- But Bob, who was safer, still makes a small profit every year. Note Risky investments don't always work out but be aware of the risk before going into anything

So how much risk should you take with your money?

Where would you put yourself on the scale 1 being not a risk taker- 10 being a big risk taker

1 - 2 - 3 - 4 - 5 - 6 - 7 - 8 - 9 - 10

Hate taking risk
(rather play it safe) ----------------→ Love taking risk

"If you had a friend with an idea for a burger stand, and he needed $25,000, would that be a good investment?"

You might say 'No'. His burger stand sounds too big of a risk. It might fail as there is too much competition already. And I'm not too sure he knows how to run a business. So, I could say there is too much risk for too little reward."

But what if I told you that your friend has previous experience in the restaurant industry and knows every aspect of the business? He has also done a lot of research on the location?

That certainly helps knowing your friend's background and decreases the risk to get the reward

SAVINGS ACCOUNT

A safe and easy way to save your money is with a bank savings account. A bank savings account allows you to deposit money or withdraw money (remove money from your account) at any time.

In return for keeping your money at the bank, the bank pays you money, also known as interest. The bank pays you for depositing money. Each bank may pay a different amount of interest, so it makes sense to look at several banks to decide which one to use.

The bank will calculate how much money you should receive in interest. As well as provide written statements of transactions (purchases, withdrawals, deposits) and account balances.

For example, if you have $100 and save it in a bank savings account, and the bank pays 5% interest, then in one year you will have an extra $5.00 in interest, or $105 in total. Therefore, the bank paid you $5.00 for saving your money with them.

For each of the following beginning savings balances and interest rates, finish filling in the following table. Round each calculation to the nearest cent.

	BEGINNING SAVINGS	INTEREST RATE	INTEREST	SAVINGS IN ONE YEAR
1.	$50.00 X	2%	$1.00	$_____
2.	$200.00 X	5%	$10.00	$_____
3.	$60.00 X	8%	$4.80	$_____
4.	$260.00 X	1%	$2.60	$_____
5.	$220.00 X	7%	$15.40	$_____

ANSWERS: 1.) 51 2.) 210 3.) 64.80 4.) 262.80 5.) 235.40

The previous calculation is called Simple interest, that, does not build up over time. Once you pay (or earn) interest for a particular period, it's gone.

Compound Interest is interest that is added to the next payment similar to a snowball that's rolling downhill. As it picks up momentum over time, it gets bigger and bigger.

Albert Einstein said "Compound Interest is the 8th wonder of the world. He who understands it, earns it; he who doesn't, pays it."

There are many ways to make a profit from compound interest. You could buy

- GOVERNMENT BOND, (YOU LEND MONEY TO THE GOVERNMENT)
- CERTIFICATE OF DEPOSIT CD FROM A BANK. -- YOU LEND MONEY TO BANKS
- CORPORATE BONDS. -- YOU LEND MONEY TO COMPANIES

These are just a few ways. Let's say you invest your money in buying a government bond

Government bond - $1,000, and - 10% a year in interest. After one year, you'd have $1,100 - (the original money plus $100 interest that you earned.)

The second year, you'd have slightly more money - $1,210 - because you're earning interest on top of interest.

The investment compounds, or builds up, over time. Now $1,210 doesn't seem like a big deal at first, but it becomes a big deal later. If we leave that $1,000 alone for 40 years, and it compounds annually at 10%, it will grow to a sum of over $53,000! And all you put in was $1,000!

Its best to start early - If you invested $10,000 today it will grow

COMPOUND INTEREST CHART

	4%	8%	12%	16%
10 YEARS	$14,802	$21,589	$31,058	$44,114
20 YEARS	$21,911	$46,610	$96,463	$194,608
30 YEARS	$32,434	$100,627	$299,600	$858,500
40 YEARS	$48,010	$217,245	$930,510	$3,787,212
50 YEARS	$71,067	$469,016	$2,890,022	$16,707,038

Michael, Jennifer, Sam all invested $1000 per month for 10 years at 7% interest.

$120,000 invested for 10 years

Michael started at age 25 – 35

Jennifer started at age 35 – 45

Sam started at age 45 – 55

By age 65, look at the figures

Michael – $1,444,969

Jennifer – $734,549

Sam – $373,407

Do you see how important it is to start early?
Everyone invested the same amount compounding at 7%.

Michael just started 20 years earlier, so by aged 65, he is a millionaire.

As you can see Time is money!
Start early – so it pays to start early

CREDIT AND INTEREST

Have you ever borrowed money? Lending and borrowing money are big parts of growing up. At some point in your life you will either lend or borrow money. Perhaps you may want to get a student loan when you finish high school and want to go to university. Or maybe you need to borrow money when you buy your first house.

Loans are valuable financial tools when they are used wisely. But loans can also get you into a lot of trouble. Loans are expenses. Remember your income must ALSO be greater than your expenses. Taking too many loans, or loans that charge high interest rate can be very bad.

When someone has money to spare, they can loan it out to someone else. In order to make it worth their while to do so, they charge interest. Interest is a percentage rate that specifies how much the borrower pays to borrow the loan.

Scenario: You have $3000 saved up but you want to make more money
- You find someone to lend money to -

Paul didn't have savings and his car broke down. Now he can't get to work.

You offer him a loan and you charge 10% interest a year

Paul pays you back the $3000 + 10% every year. Paul saved his income and had the money in 6 months meaning Paul paid $3000 +10% for 6 months =$3150.

You made a $150 profit just for having spare money!

There are risks when taking out a loan. such as, having a financial set back like losing your job. Then you will not be able to pay back the money your borrowed.

What happens if you take out a loan? Let's say to buy a jet ski but then can't afford to pay it back because you lost your job, or ran out of money?

When getting a loan, the bank or lender may ask you to secure it. This means they will ask for collateral

Collateral is an asset you have that has value. You will the asset to the lender just in case you don't pay the money back.

So to get the loan in the first place you had to tell the bank or lender you have an asset like a house, which you can use to secure the loan. Since you cannot afford the loan anymore the bank will take away your jet ski. and also your house to pay themselves the money that you owe.

OOPS...

This is why learning about this stuff now is super important. Many grown-ups who become successful can lose everything if they are not careful.

You can also get loans without securing it. (having no collateral to offer) These loans charge higher interest repayments and also have bad consequences if you cannot pay the money back, like the bank or lender taking you to court to try and get their money back.

Because you have to pay interest, you should only borrow money if the potential reward of the loan outweighs the risk of interest would have to pay.

Here is a story of taking a loan, that paid off:

ALIENWARE

Alex and Nelson wanted to make super computers for Gamers. These gamers required their computer to be fast with high graphics. It was 1996 at the time and this was not easy to find. So Alex and Nelson thought to launch Alienware.

Alex and Nelson agreed that the "risk-to-reward" ratio of getting a $10,000 loan was worth it. After a tough first year, they received great reviews of their products, and became an established brand. By 2006 revenue was in excess of 100 Million

Did you know credit cards are loans too? When you apply for a credit card you borrow money from the credit card company to make a purchase. At the end of the month, you are presented with a bill for all the purchases that you made that month.

If you pay this off in full, you will not owe any interest.

However, if you don't pay it off in full, you will be charged interest until you do. And a lot of interest too. While a home loan charge 4% interest a credit card purchase could charge up to 25%.

You will also pay money if you are late or missed a payment. As you can see, it is very easy to get yourself in big trouble quickly. Most of the time it is better not to owe anyone.

Pick the scenarios:

1 You love to sing and want to be a famous musician. You have a job delivering newspapers earning $50 a week. Its costs $1000 to record an album to send to a record producer who could possibly sign you.

2 You look after other people's pet animals at your home, while they are gone on holiday. You make a profit already by charging them per day. Business is going well. Soon there are too many dogs to handle. There is a property with a big yard for rent nearby which is really expensive to rent at $15,000 per year.

3 You just got your driver's license. Yeh! You work a part time job working in a pizza restaurant, earning around $190 per week. Getting to work takes really long and is expensive – 2 hours by bus, then half hour by train. You decide that it is time to get a car. Your neighbour has a $4000 Toyota Yaris for sale.

What are the risks of getting a loan

1. _____
2. _____
3. _____

What are the rewards of getting a loan

1. _____
2. _____
3. _____

INVENTION VS INNOVATION

Not all entrepreneurs start businesses that are on the cutting edge of technology. For every tech start-up, there are dozens of successful entrepreneurs running traditional businesses like dry cleaners, grocery stores, and mechanic shops. However, because of their independence, many entrepreneurs are able to try out new things and products.

In this area, entrepreneurs engage in either invention or innovation.
An invention is a product that is completely new.

An innovation is an improvement to an existing product, something that improves its use. For all you hear about inventions, innovations are actually far more common, but both are very important engines to drive economic growth.

Lets take a break, and do something fun, which could lead you to becoming a world famous innovator like Elon Musk. Or inventor, like Thomas Edison.

- An Invention is coming up with a new idea, or product that could change the world
- An innovation is an improvement on an idea or product, that also could change the world

In the space below draw an invention you came up with

Now in the space below Innovate something
eg. Curtains that close themselves

"Do it now sometimes later becomes never"

NEGOTIATION

What is negotiation? Have you ever wanted something, but when you asked, that person just came back with a 'NO'? That process is called negotiation. You will always be negotiating for things throughout your life, from asking to go over to a friend's house, to negotiating the price of a car when you are older.

The better you are at negotiating, it means getting your way more often. It also builds your dream life. So increase your superhero talents and I will give you tips on negotiation skills.

 **TIP 1**   "PUT YOURSELF IN THE ANOTHER PERSON'S SHOES"

If you ask your mom for a new toy she might say no. However, put yourself in your mom's shoes. and guess what she might be thinking. Maybe "my child is spoilt, he has so many toys already" or "I can't afford this"

So instead of asking for a new toy try saying "Mom I have been really good at school, All my toys are old now, may I please have this really cheap toy?"

You aren't guaranteed your mom will say yes but in her mind you aren't spoilt, the toy is cheap, and you asked nicely. She will much more likely say 'yes'

Write down how you would negotiate the following:

You want to stay up late

"Since it is a weekend
 and I don't have to be up early
 can I stay up late"

You want a new toy/watch or computer

 **TIP 2** TRY TO THINK OF WIN/WIN SITUATIONS. NOT LOSE/WIN SITUATIONS.

Both you and the person you are negotiating with want the same thing - to get a good deal. So instead of thinking I need to get my way think what can be better for both of us.

If your sister or brother wants to watch a cartoon but you want to watch a movie, instead of saying " I want to watch this movie now", be creative and think of a win/win situation say something like "if we watch 1 episode of the cartoon now, then watch a movie after, we both get what we want. Is that ok?"

Write down how you would negotiate the following

You want a sweet snack, but dinner will be soon, so you have to ask your parents

You want to watch a tv show others may not like

You do not become a professional guitarist on your first try. Practice negotiation now, it may seem small but these tips and tricks will help you negotiate your dream life. It is like negotiating a record album to signing you, or negotiating profits on a billion dollar invention.

 **TIP 3**   BE PATIENT AND CALM

Don't rush the negotiation. You might not get an answer straight away but being patient, you may end up with a better deal than you originally thought possible. Staying calm even when you don't get your way. It is important to note that when you get angry, your emotions makes you say harsh things and your thinking is not clear.

 **TIP 4**   DETERMINE THE BEST TIMING FOR THE DISCUSSION.

Think of the best time to get into negotiations with someone. Asking for a favour when someone is stressed or tired will lead to a 'no' really quick. Wait for the time when the person is relaxed, happy and not emotional.

TIP 5   IF YOU DON'T ASK, YOU DON'T GET.

Let's face it, nobody likes to be told 'no' because the fear of rejection is so strong, that leaves you stuck. The key is to remember if we don't ask, the answer will be an automatic 'no'. Even if we are told 'no', we might get a compromise (not exactly what we wanted, but close). That is better than nothing.

You have just become a famous footballer or famous actress to star in a movie. Your boss wants to negotiate your pay anywhere from $0 to $20 million. Write what you would say to him.

Tips* remember you can go play elsewhere, you have talents that no one else has and that has a price, your fans would watch you because you add value.

WHAT IS YOUR NET WORTH?

Most people have heard of assets, liabilities but what are they?
Assets: An asset is something that puts money in your pocket. It is also things of value that you own. Such as your shoes, money saved up, toys, phone etc.

Liabilities:
Liabilities are something that takes money out of your pocket (expenses) such as. if you have to pay back money you borrowed, What assets do you have? If you were to sell it second hand what would you get?

How much would you get on your

- Clothes
- Toys
- Electronics
- Money saved
- Others

What liabilities do you have?

How much do you owe?
Money would you have to pay back on:

- Fixed expenses
- Variable expenses
- Others

To calculate your net worth. Use this formula
Assets - Liabilities = Net Worth

Total assets =
Total liabilities =
Congratulations your net worth =

TAX

Have you ever wondered how schools and parks are built? Or who is in charge of paying for and maintaining roads? In short, you are! Taxes are ways that the government can collect money from its citizens to pay for things that the people need, like traffic lights and someone to pick up our rubbish.

Taxes have been around since ancient times and were sometimes paid in the form of animals since formal money had not yet been invented. Every country has different tax rules. E.g. the highest income tax you pay in Guatemala is 7% while the highest income tax for Israel is 50%!

It costs a lot of money to run a country and that is why we need to pay taxes. Most common taxes people pay.
Buy things = sales tax,
work = income tax,
Own property = property tax,
Make a profit on the stock market = capital gains tax

1. If you buy a game for $20 your sales tax is 10% (Some countries have tax included in the price, some calculate the tax at the register) 20.00 + 10% = total

    When you make money working, the government takes a percentage of your income to pay for things like having clean water come out of the taps.

2. If your pay check is $2000 and you live in Guatemala what would your net pay be?
$2000 - 7% =   tax

3. What about if you lived in Israel?
$2000 - 50% =   tax

    Often when you earn a small amount the government will take a smaller tax %, than someone that earns a lot more. This just means rich income earners contribute a lot more to the government than poor people.

Answers:
1. $2 Tax, $22 For Game
2. $140 tax, $1860 net pay
3. $1000 tax, $1000 net pay

SAD REASONS WHY PEOPLE GIVE UP

Why do some people become successful, achieving their dreams, and not everyone? Well, life gets really hard and some people sadly give up. But you are a superhero and, superheroes know battling the enemy is hard. Sometimes you have to jump high, climb mountains, dodge fire and fight through pain. Let's give your inner superhero some more power and look at obstacles you will face to reach success.

Have you ever dreamed of becoming something or doing something that seems hard, but stopped because you might fail or others will laugh at you?

Circle Yes/No

 " People laugh at your dreams because they don't have any"

 "Fear of failure, and judgment from people around them kill dreams. Superheroes fear nothing"

Do you change your dreams based on what family/friends say?

Circle Yes/No

 "Don't let someone who gave up on their dreams talk you out of yours"

 "Don't give other people the power to decide what you will become"

When doing something you are interested in like singing or riding a bike, but after you failed or things got hard did you stop and never tried again?

Circle Yes/No

 "You only fail when you stop trying"

 "If you stop walking, how do you expect to get to where you want to go?"

Do you sometimes think you cannot do or achieve something?

Circle Yes/No

 "Believe in yourself and you are half way there"

 "When times are tough, you always have to say to yourself... you're a superhero ya know!"

Have you ever been around people who you thought more fun but could get you into trouble?

Circle Yes/No

 "You can't fly high like an eagle when you hang out with turkeys"

 "Superheroes hang out with other superheroes not villains who get into trouble all the time."

Do you complain when things go wrong rather than work on solutions?

Circle Yes/No

 "When things go wrong, be grateful that a lot of things are going right"

 "Superheroes don't complain when they are losing battles. They think of solutions to come back stronger"

Does not knowing if something will work out for you, scares you enough not try?

Circle Yes/No

 "You miss 100% of the shots you don't take"

 "Not sure if you will ever save and change the world? Neither do superheroes, but that doesn't stop them from trying"

Are you unwilling to change your attitude and personality?

Circle Yes/No

 "When we improve our personality everything around us becomes better"

 "Superheroes update their weapons to be better equipped in battles. Always update and improve your personality"

Sometimes you believe in yourself and your talents but sometimes you don't?

Circle Yes/No

 "Nothing is perfect that's why pencils have erasers, so keep trying"

 "Your inner villain sometimes gets strong with negativity, crush and defeat it. Your dreams are at stake"

PERSISTENCE

Stephen was a boy who loved to write. Growing up in Maine, USA, he would dream that one day he would be a famous author. His mother was encouraging and paid him 25 cents per short story he could write. Stephen wrote and wrote getting better and better. He believed in himself that there was no way he would do anything else for a living. Writing is what he thought he was good at and he would make a living from it. True to himself Stephen held onto his dream as he grew into a teenager. He wrote his first horror book called "In a Half World of Terror", and it was published in a free magazine. Sadly, no publisher would publish the book he wrote. Unfazed, he continued to seek out any publisher who would listen. The rejection letters piled up. None of his books managed to get published.

All of Stephen's books got rejected by publishers. When Stephen reached 24 years of age, he got married. Soon he had two children to support. To make an income, Stephen worked in a laundry, only writing part time. Not being able to afford a house the family of 4 lived in a trailer. Stephen was definitely struggling and couldn't afford a telephone. Stephen focused on negative self-talk. They then settled for a below average life. When you are chasing dreams you will face obstacles and setbacks. That is certain.

You get to a point when the negative self-talk says "I'm useless, this is never going to work". Then you give up. Once you give up on something challenging your brain gets used to giving up. So the next time you do something challenging or face a setback. you give up quicker

This behaviour is a trait of your inner villain who loves to stop you from achieving your dreams. So don't get used to giving up. Instead feed your superhero with power, enough power to overcome obstacles and remain positive when there is a setback.

What setbacks will you encounter with your plan to succeed? What will you do/think when they occur?

_____
_____
_____

Stephen was at the point of writing part time- as he needed to settle for a job which he hated, just to make money. He wrote a story called "Carrie"- which was about a girl with special powers. Stephen wasn't happy with his book so he threw the papers in the bin. His wife took it out of the bin and encouraged him to finish it. The book got published! Selling over 1 million copies in its first year.

The money Stephen made enabled him to 'upgrade' his trailer into a house, buy a new car, get a telephone and provide for his family. Even better the sales from that book allowed Stephen to publish another 55 books selling over 350 Million books worldwide! All because Stephan never gave up on obstacles and perused his dream no matter what.

"Expect problems then eat them for breakfast"

~~~~~~~~~~~~~~~~~~~~~~~~~~~~~

what thoughts/feelings does this quote mean to you"

Katy loved to sing, and dreamed one day she would become a singer. At age 15 she saved up money and travelled to Nashville in Tennessee to get experience in recording music and song writing. Katy was 100% sure this is what she wanted to do with her life and she was going to be a success. The big day came just like she dreamed and she was signed by a record label. Sadly her first album was a total flop, and the record company closed down. Katy was sad but was determined and decided to keep trying to achieve her dream.

Two more record labels dropped her saying she wasn't good enough.

After so many failures surely people would think "I suck, I should give up on my dream", " So many people have told me I'm not good enough they must be right".

You see the rich and famous aren't rich and famous because life was easy for them. They have problems, just like us. Most of the time, they are bigger problems. But the rich and famous, from a young age decided to believe in themselves no matter what! Despite so many rejections katy kept making music and finely in 2007 came out with a hit song 'I Kissed a Girl'.

Now Katy Perry's net worth is $125 million. She has sold over 100 million copies of her albums.

Named Billboard magazine Woman of the Year, and recognized all over the world!

Imagine if she gave up after getting dropped?

Name a time in your life you believed you could do something, and never gave up.

"TOUGH TIMES DON'T LAST, TOUGH PEOPLE DO"

Write what thoughts and Feeligns come to mind.

About the Author

Revern (Rev) gave up on all of his vivid dreams by his late 20s and continued to live with no purpose or goals. Losing everything multiple times there was no fight left in the dog. As a last attempt, he was shipped off to Bali, where intensive care from a professional team stepped in. Years of research by experts ensued to identify where
and why people go wrong in life.

It was then the years of struggles endured by the author became 'worth the pain', in order to assist youth to never lose faith that dreams will become reality through DreamChasers.

Copyright © 2020 Revern Avin Somai

All rights reserved. No part of this publication may be reproduced, distributed, or transmitted in any form or by any means, including photocopying, recording, or other electronic or mechanical methods, without the prior written permission of the publisher, except in the case of brief quotations embodied in critical reviews and certain other noncommercial uses permitted by copyright law. For permission requests, write to the publisher, addressed "Attention: Permissions Coordinator," at the address below.

ISBN: 978-0-646-82318-8

Any references to historical events, real people, or real places are used fictitiously. Names, characters, realpeople, and places are products of the author's imagination. As well as personal perception.

All illustrations including cover done by Waywan.

Printed by Ingramspark

Ingram Spark, First printing edition 2020

Logan City, Queensland, Australia
www.dreamchasersbook.com

www.ingramcontent.com/pod-product-compliance
Lightning Source LLC
Chambersburg PA
CBHW040244010526
44107CB00065B/2864